The BUS RIDE That CHANGED HISTORY

The Story of Rosa Parks

For Mary Jane and Henry, who care about all people.
With admiration.
—Pam

For Ren
—D

Text copyright © 2005 by Pamela Duncan Edwards
Illustrations copyright © 2005 by Danny Shanahan

www.hmhbooks.com

The text of this book is set in Agenda.

Library of Congress Cataloging-in-Publication Data
Edwards, Pamela Duncan.
The bus ride that changed history : the story of Rosa Parks / Pamela Duncan Edwards ;
illustrator, Danny Shanahan.
p. cm.
HC ISBN-13: 978-0-618-44911-6
PA ISBN-13: 978-0-547-07674-4
1. Parks, Rosa, 1913 — Juvenile literature. 2. African Americans — Alabama — Montgomery — Biography — Juvenile literature.
3. Civil rights workers —Alabama — Montgomery — Biography — Juvenile literature. 4. Montgomery (Ala.) — Biography —
Juvenile literature. 5. Segregation in transportation — Alabama — Montgomery — History — 20th Century — Juvenile
literature. 6. African Americans — Alabama — Montgomery — History — 20th Century — Juvenile literature.
7. Montgomery (Ala.) — Race relations — Juvenile literature. I. Shanahan, Danny, ill. II. Title.
F334.M753P38385 2005
323.092-dc22

2004009207

Printed in Singapore
TWP 10 9 8 7 6 5

The BUS RIDE That CHANGED HISTORY

The Story of Rosa Parks

PAMELA DUNCAN EDWARDS

illustrated by **DANNY SHANAHAN**

sandpiper

Houghton Mifflin Harcourt
Boston • New York

Introduction

On February 4, 1913, a baby was born in Tuskegee, Alabama, to Leona and James McCauley, a teacher and a carpenter. They named her Rosa and thought she was the most beautiful baby ever. What they didn't know was that one day Rosa would do something so brave that it would change the course of American history.

After a few years, Rosa's father moved away, so her mother took Rosa and her baby brother, Sylvester, to live on their grandparents' farm in Pine Level, Alabama. The children had fun helping around the farm, but by the time they started going to school, Rosa was well aware that black people were treated in an inferior way.

Alabama was a "Jim Crow" state. Jim Crow laws and attitudes kept black people and white people separate and made it illegal or dangerous for black people to use the same facilities and services as white people. Black children had to go to different schools, and their parents often had to build those schools themselves. Black children were not allowed to ride a school bus with white children. In towns that did not have a bus for them, black children would have to walk to and from school. Jim Crow affected everyone, young and old. There were even white men who dressed in long robes with hoods to hide their faces. They were the Ku Klux Klan, and they rode about terrorizing black people and sometimes even killing them. Rosa lived in dread of the Klan arriving at her grandfather's farm. This never happened, but it was a scary way for a little girl to grow up.

When she was nineteen, Rosa married Raymond Parks. They lived in Montgomery, Alabama, where Rosa enjoyed setting up a home and finding a job. However, she never accepted the unjust laws against black people, and she joined lots of organizations that worked to make things better. Then, on December 1, 1955, she took a huge step toward getting one of these laws overturned. Rosa refused to stand up on a bus so that a white passenger could sit down . . .

This is a law forbidding
black people to sit next to white people on buses,
which was overturned because one woman was brave.

That's just one of the segregation laws that keep black people and white people separate.

This is a bus in Montgomery, Alabama,
where they enforced a law forbidding
blacks to sit next to whites on buses,
which was overturned because one woman was brave.

Black people pay fares at the front. Then they have to get off and go to the back to get on again!

These are the black passengers riding
the bus in Montgomery,
where they enforced a law forbidding
blacks to sit next to whites on buses,
which was overturned because one woman was brave.

This is the white man left standing near the seats of
the black passengers riding
the bus in Montgomery,
where they enforced a law forbidding
blacks to sit next to whites on buses,
which was overturned because one woman was brave.

This is the driver who told them to move for the white man
left standing near the seats of black passengers riding
the bus in Montgomery,
where they enforced a law forbidding
blacks to sit next to whites on buses,
which was overturned because one woman was brave.

This is Rosa Parks, who said, "No!" to

the driver who told her to move for the white man

left standing near the seats of black passengers riding

the bus in Montgomery,

where they enforced a law forbidding

blacks to sit next to whites on buses,

which was overturned because one woman was brave.

This is the verdict of "Guilty!" at the trial of
Rosa Parks, who said, "No!" to
the driver who told her to move for the white man
left standing near the seats of black passengers riding
the bus in Montgomery,
where they enforced a law forbidding
blacks to sit next to whites on buses,
which was overturned because one woman was brave.

This is the boycott triggered by
the verdict at the trial of
Rosa Parks, who said, "No!" to
the driver who told her to move for the white man
left standing near the seats of black passengers riding
the bus in Montgomery,
where they enforced a law forbidding
blacks to sit next to whites on buses,
which was overturned because one woman was brave.

Dr. Martin Luther King, Jr., is leading the bus boycott. He says, "We are tired . . . of being segregated and humiliated."

This is the Supreme Court ruling that declared
Alabama's race laws to be illegal, following
the boycott triggered by
the verdict at the trial of
Rosa Parks, who said, "No!" to
the driver who told her to move for the white man
left standing near the seats of black passengers riding
the bus in Montgomery,
where they enforced a law forbidding
blacks to sit next to whites on buses,
which was overturned because one woman was brave.

This is the civil rights movement, which grew in strength after
the Supreme Court ruling that declared
Alabama's race laws to be illegal, following
the boycott triggered by
the verdict at the trial of
Rosa Parks, who said, "No!" to
the driver who told her to move for the white man
left standing near the seats of black passengers riding
the bus in Montgomery,
where they enforced a law forbidding
blacks to sit next to whites on buses,
which was overturned because one woman was brave.

Black and white people are marching everywhere in the country, demanding equality for all races.

This is our country, which learned that all races are equal, because of
the civil rights movement, which grew in strength after
the Supreme Court ruling that declared
Alabama's race laws to be illegal, following
the boycott triggered by
the verdict at the trial of
Rosa Parks, who said, "No!" to
the driver who told her to move for the white man
left standing near the seats of black passengers riding
the bus in Montgomery,
where they enforced a law forbidding
blacks to sit next to whites on buses,
which was overturned because one woman was brave.

Author's Note

Rosa Parks was honored many times for her brave act. The Montgomery street where she sat down on the bus and refused to move is now named Rosa Parks Boulevard. She was given honorary degrees by universities and had a school in Detroit named for her. In 1996, she was presented with the Presidential Medal of Freedom. Three years later, the United States Congress decided that she also deserved the Congressional Medal of Freedom. This is the highest honor that Congress can give.

Sometimes it just takes one person to be brave.

DATES TO REMEMBER

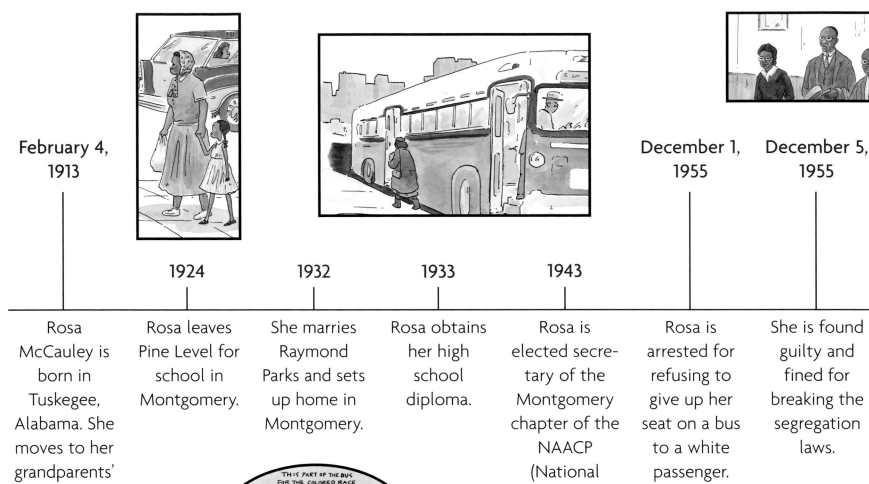

February 4, 1913

Rosa McCauley is born in Tuskegee, Alabama. She moves to her grandparents' farm in Pine Level when she is a toddler.

1924

Rosa leaves Pine Level for school in Montgomery.

1932

She marries Raymond Parks and sets up home in Montgomery.

1933

Rosa obtains her high school diploma.

1943

Rosa is elected secretary of the Montgomery chapter of the NAACP (National Association for the Advancement of Colored People).

December 1, 1955

Rosa is arrested for refusing to give up her seat on a bus to a white passenger.

December 5, 1955

She is found guilty and fined for breaking the segregation laws.

November 13, 1956

December 21, 1956

1999

Also on December 5, 1955

1957

1987

1996

The bus boycott begins.

The Supreme Court declares segregation on Montgomery buses to be unconstitutional.

The bus boycott ends.

Rosa moves to Detroit, Michigan, and continues to support the civil rights movement.

She opens the Rosa and Raymond Parks Institute for Self-Development.

Rosa receives the Presidential Medal of Freedom from President Clinton.

Rosa is awarded the Congressional Medal of Freedom, the highest honor Congress can give.

Rosa Parks
February 4, 1913–
October 24, 2005

"Love, not fear, must be our guide."
—Rosa Parks